An
Accidental
Monk

An Accidental Monk

her domestic search for God

By Marylee Mitcham

Nihil Obstat:
>   Rev. Hilarion Kistner, O.F.M.
>   Rev. John J. Jennings

Imprimi Potest:
>   Rev. Andrew Fox, O.F.M.
>   Provincial

Imprimatur:
>   +Daniel E. Pilarczyk, V.G.
>   Archdiocese of Cincinnati
>   March 19, 1976

The *Nihil Obstat* and *Imprimatur* are a declaration that a book or pamphlet is considered to be free from doctrinal or moral error. It is not implied that those who have granted the *Nihil Obstat* and *Imprimatur* agree with the contents, opinions, or statements expressed.

Cover and book design by Michael Reynolds.

SBN 0-912228-29-6

Printed in the U.S.A.

For that ragged little girl
who is always running
to catch up with something

Preface

This little book has grown out of my encounter with Cistercian monasticism. As the title implies, my encounter was unexpectedly intense. It began during my fourth pregnancy when I read *The Seven Storey Mountain*. I remember being brought back to that place in oneself where God makes urgent sense. He made sense so urgently that I cried for three days and then became a Catholic. I didn't really know who Jesus Christ was, but intuitively I realized that God was showing me the way to find out.

Later I came under the influence of other Cistercians besides Merton — the 11th century saints Robert, Alberic and Stephen, for instance. They founded Citeaux (the first Cistercian monastery), and to read of it is to be wonder-struck. Not satisfied with contemporary observance of the *Rule of St. Benedict,* they left their monastery, walked off into the marshy woods of Burgundy, and tried to do better. "Having thus put off the old man, they rejoiced to put on the new." They said this of themselves and I, for one, am moved by their understated joy.

In their primitive, concentrated and essential life, I accidentally discovered a particular way of being Christian, a way that made sense of my need to pray and live poorly. From the secular point of view, these inner necessities of mine have no value. Christianity gives them meaning; monasticism is giving them form.

Everyone who has read this volume in manuscript has said, in one way or another, that they were glad they knew the context in which it was written and that they wished I had said more about the concrete circumstances of my life. I can see their point. I like to read that kind of book myself. On the other hand, I wrote about what matters most to me: coming close to the sacred. The outer circumstances of my life have begun to make possible a wonderful thing that I hardly dare speak of. And yet it matters so much, I long to try. Describing how I actually live is different; I don't *long* to try — but I will say a little by way of a preface.

Four years ago my family left academic life

and moved to a "permanently loaned," 105-acre farm a few miles from the Abbey of Gethsemani in Kentucky. We were searching for God. I don't know exactly what that means, but St. Benedict knew that some people desire to give their life over to that task. A monk, he said, is a man who is *truly* searching for God. My husband and I wanted to find a way of life capable of testing the *truth* of our desire. We longed to "be made worthy of the promises of Christ," but we were finding it difficult, in our ordinary circumstances, to grapple with the side of ourselves that wasn't truly searching for God. We did not want to escape worldly responsibilities or our married vocation; if anything, we wanted to escape our escape of spiritual responsibilities!

This became more and more clear to us as we visited Gethsemani. Together and alone, we were drawn to the monastery and its traditions — I am tempted to write — "like moths to the flame." Heedless of the consequences, we publicly declared ourselves ready to start a small-scale community venture next door: we would learn to live with other families; we would learn to say the Divine Office; we would devote ourselves to manual labor, interior prayer and voluntary poverty. I never thought about hospitality but that turned out to be an indispensible Christian virtue, so we tried.

Christ has continued to speak to us through the spirit of the Cistercians. The monks, of course, don't raise children or live in nuclear families with a spouse. But by their penance and seclusion, by their austere effort to prefer nothing to the love of Christ, they have spoken past our obvious differences.

Presently we live with two other families. Each family has its own (non-electric) house, its own part-time job and economy, and its own identity. But we do share prayers three times a day, rising at 4 a.m. and getting to bed by 8:45 p.m., if we're lucky. We work together on our small farm (cow, chickens, big garden) and the construction of our dwellings, and we gather for business and formation meetings. Our children ride a school bus to the nearest parochial school. They seem to be thriving. Although we don't assume our children will adopt the life we have chosen, the fact that they prosper is for us one of the clearest signs that we should continue.

We are not connected with the Abbey in any official way; it is more like we have lots of spiritual fathers down the road. The monks have consistently shown us the face of Christ. Others have too, of course, for once you begin to see it, you see it lots of places. I know it is everywhere. Perhaps with more time, I will come to know in a deeper way. For now, I learn to see it close at home.

"Can you believe it?" Carl and I ask ourselves again and again. "Can you believe what God has done for us?" He provides the candle, lets us fly into it, and uses the ash to make signs of mercy across our commonplace life.

Marylee Mitcham

The Feast of St. Angela Merici, 1976

I

Being a convert to Catholicism has its advantages—one doesn't have to shed as much of one's past as a cradle Catholic does these days. Since I strip by temperament anyway, I don't find my advantage to lie in having escaped the grief of leaving things behind; I simply mean being a convert has saved me a certain amount of time because I was relatively empty to begin with. Not much was alive in those rooms which I occupied, but at least they weren't full of unnecessary furniture.

I have come upon my religious life like one comes upon a clearing in the woods. The grace of God has given me space and a cottage to set up housekeeping and the grace of God slowly provides me with the simple accoutrements I need to live. There are others who must go about their house-cleaning, but it seems to me that with my entry into the Church, I have been given a fresh beginning. It was out of the dark into the light and the light, being truly simple, is at times overwhelming.

"It is a terrible thing to fall into the hands of the Living God." Besides being a stripper, I am a writer on kitchen walls; and for two years those words lived on my wall and in my heart. I have been in the Church six years now and I have come to know a little of her riches. It astounds me to enter at a time when others are leaving. I do not understand. What little I know suggests to me that the Church, too, is a stripper, but it is a matter far too complex for me. Or I should say, the spirit that informs this particular matter is beyond my scope. I concentrate on the small, on what unfolds in my way within the Way. I am merely a wife, a mother of four, a friend to some, and an accidental monk.

I have received a call to my accidental vocation—that much is sure. I know I have received it because I experience the grace that flows from my struggle to answer that call. Grace

8

flows when I agree to struggle with it at some unspecified future time. Grace even flows when I simply think about trying. Whatever small amount of consent I offer, I am generously rewarded. But the struggle itself is never consoling; it always feels hard and lonely and beyond me. I could say it this way: my consent feels like leaving home; God's grace feels like coming home; the struggle to be faithful to a call feels like being outside in the weather.

II

Good news was announced through my husband about 10 years ago in the slums of San Francisco. He painted the first kitchen sign which said, "Less is more." How those words settled in and satisfied my spirit! Neither of us had left all things to follow Christ, but we were mercifully unconformed to the plentiful time and wanted to live out what little we knew. The miracle is that the little we knew was more. Over the years our kitchen sign branched out like the mustard seed so that what was once only a grain of insight has now become a whole life and we are called to the seen and unseen poverty of the Kingdom of God. I emphasize the word *called*. Human nature is slow to respond.

Driving to the Laundromat, This Poem:

Full of practical efficiency and, yes, devotion
She straightens up her house with no commotion.
And if the fire burns low, there is no shame
For God wraps human nature in a flame.

III

One thinks of monks as hidden men. Hidden from whom? Certainly not from God for whom "night is as bright as day." But they are hidden from the world, yes. And also hidden to some extent from each other. In what sense? It is this way: having given all they have to God, they must leave it to him to give them back what they need. And God, not being a Pharisee, never sounds trumpets when he gives alms. He is a secret giver, a patron known only to the poor men he supports.

For their part, they would gladly tell others their good news; but being poor, they hold little interest for the world. "So," says the world, "you have a patron, hmm? He replenishes your poverty, I see. Let me know when he replenishes your wealth!" Like it or not, then, monks are hidden—but they are not in hiding.

IV

"What do you write about, Mama?"
"Oh, I write about God and houses."

What *is* my obsession with houses? I used to
be very attached to the idea of home but now,
uprooted in spirit, I am voluntarily homeless.
Yet I am still attached to the Garden House,
the house where I live. My husband finds it
significant to build houses and I find it significant to be in them. The main thing is that they
enclose space. Enclosure and space. Both reali-
ties strain to make themselves clear in my mind.
They speak to me of something more—discipline and prayer. All of a sudden it makes sense.
Walls discipline space and space is that empty
stretch of silent prayer, that free-flowing longing and peace found within.

How amazing it seems! There are two pictures hanging in my house side by side. One is
a house and one is a prairie. Only now, as I
write, do I understand their meaning for me.
They have hung there a year and a half waiting
for me to see them.

I keep trying to find a book for my children
that I loved when I was about nine years old.
It's called *The Boxcar Children* and is one of
the first glimmers of my accidental vocation.
I don't remember the plot, only that four children were left suddenly on their own and they
set up housekeeping in an abandoned boxcar.
It appealed to me in every way: their self-reli-
ance, their poverty, their hidden lives. And of
course the boxcar—a house, an enclosure.

So here I sit in the very small house my husband built from scavenged materials. Like its
occupants, it is unfinished and crude: potbelly
stove, buckets of water, a broom and no toilet.
It is just right for me—will help me seek God.
I love it like a child, which means I'm not
above griping at it. It puts everything on the
floor, this house! But because we live so cramp-
ed, my husband is building me a room of my
own in the form of a hermitage 8′ x 12′. A
boxcar for one. An empty room where hopefully the Spirit can "well in my heart," as six-
year-old Emily says.

V

For some reason, it's very hard to think of enclosures as places where anything truly important can take place. They rub. They seem a waste. And in one sense that is true. Like the desert to which monks have been called for centuries, enclosures are wastelands. They have to be, or else those who live in them would put down roots and become part of the world again.

As a woman, I am familiar with enclosures, being one myself. Nobody ever put down roots in my womb—my babies left me for the world! But much that was important took place in me. Nevertheless, the thought of containment is frightening even to those who see the value in it. As Americans (as human beings?) our longing for freedom automatically prompts us to break out of things. It takes time and patience to consider freedom in terms of living peacefully "within"—freedom seen not as the possibility of escape but as a kind of stability, akin to monastic stability. It's easy to say but hard to do. That's why God must call us to it.

As a Christian I am told that freedom is being where the Spirit of the Lord is, which means being in some sense "within"; for the Kingdom of God was not said to be "without." And if God's mercy is "mercy within mercy within mercy," then how shall we find it if we are always afraid of being trapped inside, as it were?

The secret, I think, lies in understanding that enclosure is hardly a dead end. It is more like those Chinese boxes that fit cleverly one inside another; enclosure within enclosure, with the tiniest inward box being the infinitely large face of God.

One night in a dream I felt cheated because I could not be inside the monastery. I cried and railed and asked Thomas Merton how I was to grow, being stranded outside. His answer was comforting: "You will. Your vocation will unfold on its own. There are other enclosures." Now I am able to recognize some of them—to walk the perimeters. At times I struggle with the desire to break out. Marriage is a good example. Like a monastery, marriage doesn't keep you in unless you agree to let it, but then, does it ever! There are other walls too. The commotion and crowding of family life are sturdy limits within which your prayer must be born (or stillborn).

VI

My daughter Jessica had a house dream when she was six years old that I will never forget. There were two enclosures: her house (where she was taking refuge from witches) and a wooden box inside her house. She lifted the

Come adore Christ our Lord!♥

be Kind

★ ALLELUIA!

Christ has risen!

Love and serve him

Jessica Mitcham

lid of the box and there was Christ. "Do not be afraid," he told her. "If the witches touch you they will die. But if you touch them, you will die."

Irritated, a friend recently called me a "black box." Interesting how close he came to my image of myself.

But if you open me up, will you find Christ? Am I black to my friend or am I black? I stare at my house picture on the wall. There is a light in the window. For a long time I thought it was a light inside the house and I felt somehow comforted—as though it were *my* light, *my* goodness. Then one day I realized that it came from the sun striking the windowpane and briefly I felt afraid. The house was dark after all. Its only light was from the sun.

Oh God, be merciful to me a sinner. Know that I don't want to touch witches, I don't want to be dark.

VII

Today at Mass we sang out for the martyrs who "washed their robes in the blood of the Lamb." That's a fine phrase, combining as it does the ultimate trials of faith and the housewife's task of washing clothes. It's a good image for monks who, like the martyrs, "let go" completely. But the holocaust is calm and homely.

The essential question in discerning a monastic vocation shouldn't be whether one is called to marriage or not. It should have to do with whether one is called *right now* to liberation in faith from the bonds of the world. And why should God *not* ask this of some people even after they have worldly ties? As though God only asked poor people to be "poor" and not sometimes those who live amid comfort as well. There are paradoxes. Indeed, Christianity is built on one.

And if a married couple is asked to live, like monks, prematurely unbound from the world but in a less obvious way than monks—is not this hidden reality simply another dimension of the loss and poverty to which they are invited?

VIII

Detachment is a hard thing to understand. There are several things, though, which it definitely is not: it is *not* living inside the monastery of one's own head; it is *not* being emotionally or physically invulnerable; it is *not* doing without everything you care about; and it is *not* the knack of conforming smoothly to every situation. At one time or another, I have tried to make it all four of these and all I can say is, it is *not*.

As for what it is, about all I really know is this: it is a gift and that's why it is hard to understand ahead of time. Like humility, you can't go out and "do it." The best one can do is pray for it and then add a little weight to the issue by beginning to practice renunciation more feelingly. That's sort of like saying, till it hurts. It won't take much. You don't have to renounce everything that you hope one day to leave behind—that effort would be better spent meditating on what it means to "hope." No, renounce something of no importance; something trivial and hard like solid food for 24 hours. It's amazing what a chunk that may take out of you. All day long you'll feel a little lost and disoriented, sort of like someone just asked

21

you a question but you forgot what it was.

It's just that kind of empty feeling that can work wonders. If you resist the immediate temptation to drink milk shakes, you will almost certainly learn something about yourself—usually something trivial (and hard).

But getting back to detachment: it begins to come later on, after numerous good-hearted renunciations. God asks you a question and, lo, you don't feel lost or disoriented. You may feel empty, but you remember the question and are able to reply.

Detachment can be a tricky thing if you've got a natural pull to the inner world anyway. We each have our own Screwtape and mine has tried many times to lure me away from reality.

I remember reading a short story by Doris Lessing long ago that left me shaking for—well, years maybe. It was about an initially sane, ordinary woman who irrationally, yet deliberately withdrew from her family, lured by something that eventually took shape as a little man. She let her husband assume she had a lover, but actually she was spending more and more time alone in a cheap hotel room lying down. She distanced herself from them so cleverly that they never suspected the truth and then, as could be expected, she distanced herself from

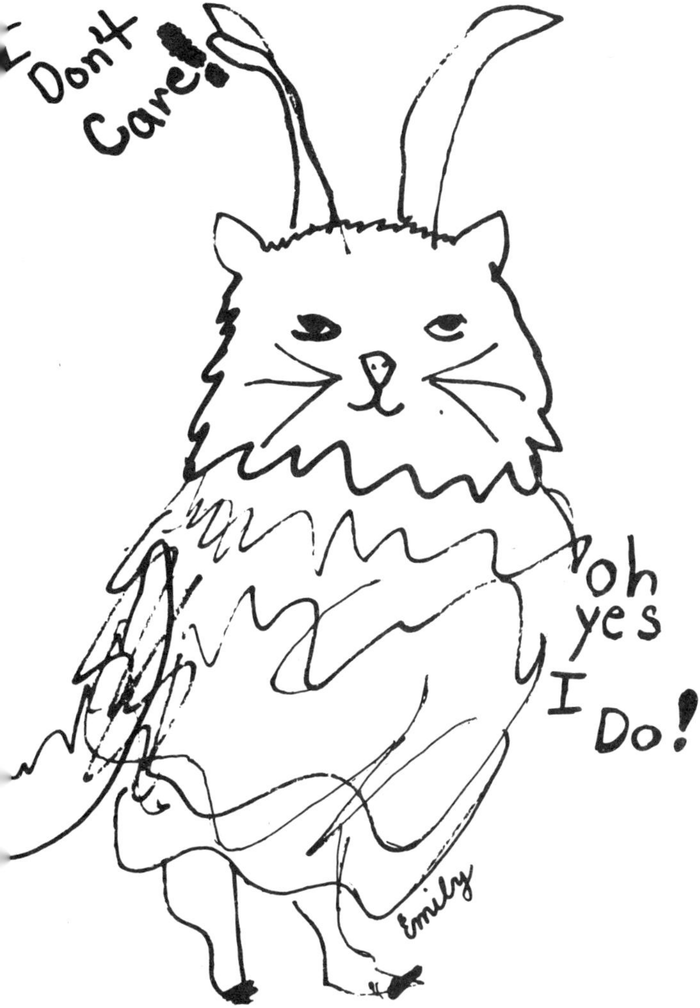
I Don't Care!
oh yes I Do!
Emily

herself and deliberately died. I vaguely realized that "If I do it wrong, that's how it will be." Funny thing, too, because I had no conscious thoughts about doing anything, let alone doing something right. But I was being called, even before I was a Christian, to a life of detachment.

I kept remembering that story off and on. I can only call the memory Providential because at one point I was wrestling with exterior reality and felt greatly frustrated.

The temptation was to escape interiorly. And, indeed, Christ did say "come" in a clear and compelling way. But he also said "go" in the next instant. I was deeply confused. It was as though he motioned and urgently signaled me to come only to whisper in my ear when I obeyed, "Why aren't you out there where you were when I beckoned?" It didn't seem fair. But the story helped me understand.

A genuine call unites "come" and "go." It doesn't say "inner *or* outer"; it says "inner *and* outer." He is within it *all.* We are invited to live with him within it all. Christ never leads us away from reality—he gives us another portion of reality thus making our life abundant.

IX

Coming and going makes me think of that first Lent and Easter. It was penance that drew me into the Church because I knew how to cooperate with death better than life.

I suppose it's more usual to feel helpless in the face of death and to take life for granted as something we always have at our disposal to shape and control. In my case, though, it was "comings" that made me feel helpless. They happened every moment all around me. I lived upheld by a stream of comings in an utterly mysterious way; only in "going" did I seem to control my life. So that first year as a Catholic I channeled my enthusiasm for the incoming tide into a great enthusiasm for mortification, the outgoing tide.

Easter morning I expected nothing, but as soon as I walked through the church doors I knew Christ was rising. He was coming, but not in my own heart yet; it seemed I was just looking on. I was like the woman at the well whose response to Christ was a surprised and excited leave-taking. She wanted most of all to go tell others whom she had seen.

In the Car Again, This Image:

I always expected
    a deluge of endings
        but found instead
            the mouth of the spring.

I can't help it, I am a believer in asceticism. That is not to say I am a great ascetic (one lost dream). I have learned there are many disciplines I cannot bear. Nevertheless, I continue to put on what asceticism I can because, like clothing, it's practical. Originally it served as some sort of moral corset worn to support my sagging will. It set a tone of "harsh and dreadful labor" against the forces of my own sluggishness.

Now the emphasis is different. I feel that I am clothed in a robe of repentance. Ascetic discipline expresses my sorrow—widow's weeds for lost purity and moribund goodness. And I suppose it serves the same function as black: it witnesses to my sorrow but relieves me somewhat of the constant burden of *feeling* it. By casting my emotion in a form of its own, I set myself free to wait quietly. I make room for joy.

X

I'm sorry I didn't read the *Rule of St. Benedict* sooner. It is an unforgettable document—not primarily because it legislates so well but because a magnificent spirit flows from it. I expected St. Benedict's prudence but was taken by surprise at his saintliness. No dry matter, this Rule. I can see why it inspires such devotion.

My attraction to it seems strange. Yes, I know I am called to the *Opus Dei* in a spare, married context but it is more than that. There is a certain quality in the Rule that I long for in myself. To adapt what was said of a contemporary soprano: St. Benedict's voice is achingly pure-of-heart. And it sweeps. His word "breaks forth like the dawn," yet it is a dawn seen from the perspective of earth. "Let him always distrust his own frailty," he says of the Abbot. "Let him always set mercy above judgment so that he himself may obtain mercy."

The first night after reading the Rule, I dreamed about a monastery of straight lines and rough surfaces; a place in perfect, masculine control of itself. At first I was filled with admiration but then as I looked around, I felt uneasy because there was no roundness anywhere. Suddenly I caught sight of a dove sitting high on a rafter overhead. As if in answer to my growing distress, it flew down and left the building through a tiny round hole in the door. (Ah, a divine loophole!) "Only a dove could have found it," I said to myself with satisfaction.

Outlining a life profoundly lenten in character, Benedict obviously knew what it was to flounder. He realized interstices make tight structures human.

Compassion is a round virtue. It's for those who are whole (excuse the pun). It has a passive element, vulnerability, but it is full of hope which makes it active and mysteriously effective in alleviating suffering.

For years I thought compassion was kamikaze feeling, as when one is driven to provide misery her company. It was a last resort when I thought there was nothing left to do but feel pain.

XI

Anna, who is five, likes me to sing a song I wrote called, "I'm So Humble, Humble, Humble, I Don't Grumble, Grumble, Grumble." (I stole the title.) One morning she asked me to sing the part about a cup of tears, so ceremoniously I warbled, "Oh I eat my bread of ashes and I drink my cup of tears. I don't complain—it just adds misery to my years." Later that afternoon she came back and said, "Mama, I have a question. If you don't complain, where do you get the cup of tears?"

I often wonder how my accidental vocation will affect the children, especially Anna who doesn't go to school yet. I always seem to have snatches of psalms floating around in my head and Anna, likewise, is being nourished, but more haphazardly. She'll sit and draw while she sings a phrase over and over—something like, "to the least of my brethren," or "alleluia with my love." Her pictures are often religious. One of my favorites is "a lady praying to God with spiderwebs in the corner." Drawn true to life!

The children used to talk about commercials and imitated the slick women they saw on TV. Now they play Mass. Everyone wants to be priest so Anna Hosanna the Least has to be the

anna

entire congregation. Her mouth bulges with
tiddlywink hosts. "Which game is profane?"
I ask myself. A rhetorical question.

There is the Child Jesus. There is the Man Jesus. What about Mother Jesus? At least one mystic has called him that—Julian of Norwich, reputedly a shrewd spiritual mother herself. I would guess that in her own shrewdness she sensed our Lord's capacity for a mother's tricks. I have had the uncanny experience myself. At times it's quite clear to me that I am a child playing house. I am being kept busy with ascesis in much the same way that I direct my children's attention to something absorbing but harmless so I can do what needs doing.

"Oh, Marylee," the Mother Jesus in me seems to say. "Go ahead now, wash your dishes and meditate a bit. Let me do my work in peace! How can I sweep cobwebs out of your heart with you underfoot?"

Being a well-loved child, I am able to go back to my musing and in a few minutes I have lost sight of my Mother again, so absorbed am I by pretty clay dishes and funny clay men.

For Julian

Cloistered privileges and cloistered pain —
Behold the lonely access to His reign.

High understanding and inward grace —
To know the Kingly gift of anchored space.

XII

Occasionally God lets us experience our wretchedness, but don't be deceived: this is a consolation. You can tell yourself that you are face down in the dust and that you are feeling humble to the bone but, listen, you are just in the throes of awe. It's a relief to experience your total unworthiness for a change. It's a very clean feeling: a true grace. The ordinary experience of humility is not really an experience at all. There's no peak—just bedrock.

Could one say that humility is knowing you have some strength but not much? Perhaps it's understanding yourself as an ordinary person who will probably never be first *or* last. But even so, watch out! You may soon find yourself with an increased appreciation of the ordinary. Wasn't Simone Weil ordinary? No one noticed her silent sanctifying presence. Just so with your own secret riches!

Oh, it all feels so shoddy. Working at humility is a disgusting business. It's not our business at all; leave it to God. But, you know, I have it on good authority that believing God can lead you to holiness is not pride; it is believing that God is able to bring the most amazing things to pass.

XIII

At supper the other evening, our 14-year-old son, Mark, hazarded the opinion that more people aren't Christian because it's just too scary being that close to the Power of the Universe. I was struck again by the blessings heaped on our house. Christ is more tangible at times than our son approves of. His life seems to him to be complicated by a too-immediate relationship with God.

I think of a day the two of us spent in Louisville. Mark is impossibly absentminded and, in keeping with his debility, he lost a valuable library book somewhere downtown. We retraced our steps through store after store and finally, full of irritation, I asked him if he had prayed for help in finding the book. No, he hadn't; he was so disgusted with himself for losing things that he didn't think he even ought to ask.

As we walked into the last store, the last possible place, I heard Mark groan. "Now I have to give up bubblegum," he said wearily, holding the book up for me to see. "When I realized this was the last place it could be, I got weak and I told God if only he'd help me find it, I'd give up bubblegum."

God treats me with the same heavy-handed mercy sometimes. I can remember one day when all I did was worry, not pray mind you, just worry—about how I could be certain that the graces I received were real. Perhaps they were the result of an overly suggestible mind. Finally, after hours of convoluted thoughts, I did pray and the idea came to me to open the New Testament at random and ask for a word that would "speak to my condition." I did so, putting my finger on: "Ask, and you will receive. Seek, and you will find. Knock, and it will be opened to you."

This satisfied me immediately because I knew I had asked and sought and knocked many times in faith. Why should I begin to doubt when doors opened? And then, frail vessel that I am, I got greedy. I sensed very clearly that this passage from Scripture was an answer given me by the Lord. Nevertheless, I wanted more. I wanted to be told other things. Knowing how wrong I was, I didn't reopen the Bible but about half an hour later I had convinced myself that if I opened *another* book, I wouldn't have a guilty conscience. Hurriedly I took from the shelf Richard Rolle's *The Fire of Love* and opened it blindly to this: "Ask and you will receive. Everyone who asks receives, and it is opened to him who knocks."

I'm sure Mark would understand my reaction; I was scared being that close to the Power of the Universe. *God is*. He is the *I am*. He utterly sees through me. Incredibly, he indulges me.

The pattern of mercy is consistent on level after level—from the most concrete level where he literally saves us or heals our bodies to more subtle levels of understanding and knowing. What is certain is that he is everywhere that I am, that he touches me from all quarters at all times. The more still and expectant I become, the more of his mercy I see. But always he startles me. A moment ago, I knew him to be hidden within; now he is no longer hidden, he is simply within. It astonishes me. It is a fearful thing.

XIV

I wish I could remember where I read or
heard about a Zen Roshi who said one had to
be desperate to be a successful candidate for
Zen. At the time his remark struck me as likely
although I knew it sounded unlikely. There is a
wild kind of hunger for prayer and meditation
akin to desperation: a sense of urgency poorly
understood even by those who experience it.

When I read *Maria Chapdelaine,* I felt I
found a metaphor in those French-Canadian
settlers who moved into virgin forests with
their families and "made land," as they said.
Ostensibly they wanted to settle, and clearing
the dense timber by hand was the terrible
price they had to pay for space to build and
plant. In reality, though, some of them were
driven to the work of clearing itself. Once that
was accomplished they found excuses to leave
their farms and begin again. They wanted to
struggle, even die. They had to "make land"
for inexplicable reasons.

At prayer, sometimes, I settle down as
though confronting Destiny. Then I say to myself (in a mock-tough way that connects me
with my own homesteading grandparents and
ancestors): "O.K., woman. Let's make land."

And I've found those words to be powerful tools for clearing the forests of the mind.

Several times now I have heard people recommend a particular way of praying that starts from me and gradually spreads and extends to include all others. First my love encompasses my family, then my neighbors, then all Americans, then the world. It's more subtle than that of course, but that's the idea— to gradually increase the boundaries of your heart. But when I try it, I find myself almost immediately exhausted; utterly weary with a kind of disgust one feels when she has grasped for more and more and more. Indeed, the world is too much with me. I feel imprisoned by universal domestic life. I am the mother of everyone!

To widen my love, I have to loosen my grip and leave the world. Working my way from the outside limits of my heart to its center, I take leave of creation until finally I am able to pray D. H. Lawrence's poem:

> There is nothing to save, now all is lost,
> but a tiny core of stillness in the heart
> like the eye of a violet.

Then and only then, in the peace of renunciation, can I make a gift of my love to others. There is no pulling them into myself. They are not collected in my expansible heart, because my heart is small and does not expand easily. And I refuse to be a thief grabbing at valuables.

The only way I know to include everyone is to stop trying to do it long enough to see that it is already done. Christ accomplished what I cannot. Everything of mine is lost; there is nothing for me to save. There is only Salvation and the mystery of Christ's love. It touches everywhere. Sunlight in the desert.

XV

I was driving somewhere with the three girls and they were talking about what they were going to be. Six-year-old Emily said she was going to get married, be a nurse, and live in our community. Nine-year-old Jessica said she was going to get married, be a teacher, and live in our community. The five-year-old then said emphatically, "I don't want to be anything or do anything. I just want to live in our community." There was a silence while her sisters tried to figure this out and then one of them said, "Anna just wants to be herself."

Me too. I can hardly stand to hear it put that way anymore. The expression "be yourself" is as trite as the problem is commonplace. So what? At least the answer holds interest. As far as I can see, prayer is the only means for me to be myself. Until I learn to pray unceasingly, I won't act like who I am.

Who am I? A woman bound at her deepest point to Jesus Christ. Of what does my prayer consist? Of remembering who I am. What happens when I don't pray? I forget how to be myself. At least for today, it's as simple as that.

XVI

To choose marriage is normally to choose a lively womb. To choose celibacy is to choose a quiet one; to choose simplicity of body. But as the Shakers knew from experience—"tis a gift to be simple."

What does a married woman say about celibacy? That it took her a long time to appreciate it? Yes. That she is bewildered by a growing desire for sexual abstinence? Yes.

Having gladly borne children, I am awed by my own womb. It amazes me to watch my son and daughters—so whole and separate—and know that they issued from that empty place inside me. What greater natural mystery could there be? Something out of nothing. But, no, it's wrong to say that. We make that mistake so easily thinking that emptiness is "nothing," and perhaps that's one reason why celibacy was hard for me to understand.

Nothingness is such an alarming thought. Idols, for instance, are nothing. Even having mouths, they cannot speak. An evil heart is nothing; the mouth speaks but nothing flows from it. The psalms describe nothingness with all the vigor of our worst nightmares.

Indeed, if a woman did choose "nothing" when she chose celibacy, then her womb would be a void right at the center. It would be that gaping inner pit we halfway believe in as it is. Instinctively, I myself chose inner life in the form that I recognized it.

Now, looking back, I have no regrets but more must also be said (for it is the truth): Lacking the wisdom of empty wombs, I turned away from a form of poverty pregnant with beauty and grace. It takes time to love some barren places.

Useless as spent money
my passion contradicts itself
and in the stretching
    of that argument
chooses empty pockets

We build small fires
and feel the chill —
we search for paths
around the hill

XVII

Christ's work is to bring to completion the fullness of grace, and that's my work as well. In keeping with the past, I labor—bringing Christ to birth in myself. It is a long pregnancy, increasingly uncomfortable. But at the right moment death and birth coincide and Christ emerges naked and visible. We will have given birth to each other.

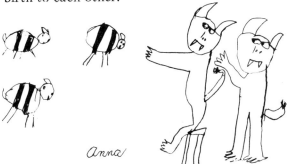

Anna

Anna to me as Emily scrubs the floor on her hands and knees: "Emily's best things are God and work. Her bad-est things are the Devil and bees. Devils don't even love! Bees love a little but not very much."

Emily: "Bees love to make honey."

Anna: "Yeah. I guess they aren't your bad-est thing, Emmy."

Mama: "What's your best thing, Anna?"

Anna: "God. I hate the Devil and work."

XVIII

The peace of Christ is like a secret we were keeping from ourselves.

Fear is a possessive old lover that I left. He was never any good and I always knew it, but only recently did I feel enough contempt for our familiarity to tell him plainly that he could never keep me. I would ignore his presence, I said; I would laugh in his face.

Pain is my illegitimate child, born from a wound. Fear smirks. He says she is growing bigger. She is growing, it is true. But I do not call her Pain anymore because he liked that name. I call her Daughter and speak to her softly. It seems to me she is growing lovely.

When she is grown, her name will be Joy and mine will be Bride. Then we will laugh together like girls about how long it took and tell homemade fables about the past.

XIX

I have dreamed about Christ many times,
but only once has he spoken to me in a dream.
I was sitting at his feet and weeping at his words,
so deeply did they move me. And I remember
them still. It is quite embarrassing because they
are so silly. He said,

"But that Christ did not pack,
will you sit utterly and listen?"

Yet, in a way, they are interesting words.
Rorshach words. My interpretation was, "Don't
sit and listen to vain philosophies—listen to me."
My husband's interpretation was more Martha-
like: "Don't just sit there packing. Get going
like me!"

XX

I believe in a husband's headship but I don't think of it as a simple thing. Or I should say, I think it's profoundly simple in the same way that perfect charity is essentially "simple" or a monastic vocation is "simple" being entirely directed toward the search for God alone. Headship, too, is something a man grows into as he becomes more profoundly simple himself. In time he learns to love his wife as Christ loves the Church. He learns to see the "more" hidden within her "less." If his eye is single, he will truly see her. He will be Head.

And just so with wife. Mystically speaking, she is Body. This is a great mystery and great mysteries do not declare their meaning crudely. Personally, the image of body appeals to me much more than the image of head. Where is the heart, but in the body? Let the head say Jesus prayers as much as it likes; until they repeat in the heart, one has scarcely begun.

"The Body of Christ"
"Amen"

XXI

I was telling Anna that God gives us our body back after death. "I know," she said with conviction. "Jesus makes the wind blow it back."

"Well, sort of," I replied. "It's kind of like the Holy Spirit blows life back into us."

She nodded and gave me one of her wise, radiant smiles before singing a verse from "My Bonnie Lies Over the Ocean":

"The winds have blown over the ocean. The winds have blown over the sea. The winds have blown over the ocean and brought back my body to me!"

"Hey, look at me, Emmy. I'm holy!" says Anna as she walks across the room with a book balanced on her head.

"Oh, Anna," comes the reply from Emily, "you're not *holy*—you're just *full of grace*."

XXII

Lawrence/Jeffers/Lowrey

Three apostates
Three married hermits

> Here I go again, praying for the
> repose of their souls. The feet in
> my heart get tired but I keep
> it up because my gratitude has
> not yet worn itself out.

> You men. I am tired of men!
> But you understood shacks—
> suitable dwellings for derelict
> souls. And in your pages, life
> rose for my sake.

Three heralds crying in this wilderness
Three strange angels

XXIII

"Life," said St. Teresa, "is but a night spent
in an uncomfortable inn, crowded together
with other wayfarers." My heart sinks at those
words—the image is so apt. Another house con-
fronts me, an enclosure. This one is an inn, not
a cell. It is an uncomfortable inn. As far as I'm
concerned, that goes without saying. In the
middle of everyone I am never comfortable.

Despite an affinity to houses, my conscious
mind rebels and searches for alternative images
of my life. A raft? Could I be on a raft with my
husband and children? Then strangers wouldn't
knock at our door. Or a road? We could travel
the road together, carrying but few provisions.

I will agree to journey at night because there
is no other way for any of us. For mankind
the day remains as dark as night. We do not

know and must suffer our fear. But must I also agree to miserable accommodations for the night when I am willing to do without accommodations at all? I will walk all night! Like the Baptist, I long to decrease—but in the desert, not in an inn. I don't agree to St. Teresa's gregarious wisdom. I can't conform voluntarily to her folly. I try to say yes unconditionally, but it sticks in my throat.

In his mercy, God accepts a half-hearted yes. I do not feel chastised, only sad and embarrassed by the regularity of my panic. Over and over again, I stumble into the inn of community life and inform everyone that it's much too crowded to spend the night. I will stay a few hours just to help out, but then I must leave the hustle and bustle. It is not for me to divide myself endlessly for those who come. It is not for me to. . .go. . .to. . .pieces. . . for. . .a. . .mere. . .vision. . .

God shields me when my senses cannot tolerate my own experience. I am quite free to pick my own metaphors, to search out other symbols. I am allowed to state my case in uncheerful, niggling words. His only response is a fond one. I wonder if he even cares what I say? Words, words—we both know our covenant goes deeper than words. How I tremble.

Community life is looking for itself in me.
I wish it would go look in someone else.

Living with you and him and her is like coming on stage for the magician's finale. Self-consciously I commit myself to the box. Swords are everywhere plunged through; jokes too. No alarm now! In a minute we will have success!

To the sound of applause, I daintily step out, demonstrating my soundness of body; soundness of heart especially.

It would spoil everyone's fun to comment on blood.

I cannot write about community. I am the soup, not the cook. The heat is on and I cannot comment.

I am at the disposal of everyone, I moan, watching greasy water run down the sink and out into the meadow beyond my window. It is only a question of disposal, I tell myself, feeling my spirit drain away.

My dreams are full of houses, of crowded inns particularly. Again and again I dream of rooms endlessly connected. No one can tell where one apartment stops and another starts. People are everywhere, restlessly opening doors and jostling each other. I seek refuge in the bathroom but it has doors on every wall. I look around and think, "What a horrible place. There is nowhere here to strike a match!" These are my horizontal dreams.

When I dream about vertical rooms, though, I am relaxed and at peace. Climbing up hidden stairs I discover an empty, charming garret apartment. In the process of exploring it, I find more stairs and an even better apartment above. And then again! There is no doubt about my inclinations. "May peace reign in your walls, in your palaces peace."

XXIV

This afternoon I woke up from a nap thinking, "sublime crime"—"sublime crime." I knew I would feel a vague anxiety for the rest of the day if I didn't allow myself time to sit quietly and reclaim the dream connected with that weighty rhyme.

So I did sit quietly and soon I realized I had been dreaming of the crucifixion and of another dreamer, Pontius Pilate's wife. She was no longer a nervous Roman matron—a woman of dread. I saw her after Christ had died. She stalked the streets of Jerusalem like one of Shakespeare's mourning women, her hair loose and face wild with grief. And I felt real pity for this creation of my own mind who also lived once. I wanted to comfort her because she is caught and hidden in a history that overlooks everything about her except a nightmare come true. Was she really born just to dream that dream?

XXV

How can one be a monk and not write about silence? But the best thing to say about silence is nothing.

I will write of next best things. It seems to me there are two kinds of silence—the one we can have and the one we want and wait on. The first is human. It is full of tiny human sounds and inner words, hopefully not profane inner words. The other silence is infinitely more real than sound. Monks know themselves to have come from it and they know themselves as going to it. To be at peace we must learn the one and adore the Other.

One trouble with words is they keep you from experiencing the present. Confronted with the present, we fumble for something to say about the past or we rush to suggest something about the future. It takes nerve to let the present disclose itself because *it* does the talking and it likes to come *asking*.

Not infrequently I am asked, "But what do you do with yourself?"

"Not much," I usually reply and wonder if I should mention how many hours it all takes. Next time I'll look my visitor right in the eye and say, "I work at being peaceful" or "I'm studying how to be content."

It is a theme that absorbs me. Those around say they even hear me talking about it to myself in the outhouse. The privy is doorless—why don't I stare peacefully into the woods and keep quiet? Like the eccentric woman who combed her hair at night to save time in the morning, my own behavior often works against me. I must learn to listen. I must learn to wait!

XXVI

Sometimes I feel exactly in the middle of
myself, and the extreme pressure of being
there—of having all the deep tensions and de-
sires in myself so tautly in a state of balance—
makes me feel, well, somehow it makes me *feel*
like I should just vanish in a puff of smoke. I
think of burnt offerings wholly consumed.

But what have I actually said spiritually? I've
merely described a sensation in biblical metaphor. I've described; I haven't understood.

I remember asking Father Flavian about this
sensation once and he replied that he had posed
the same question to Thomas Merton who said
this: "I don't know what it is but it's useless."
The longer I live with that answer, the better
it wears.

Martha and Mary

I lived through a time
when the world was too particular.
It was vertical and multiple
and, like a busy Martha,
kept engaging my attention
with an awkward mention of itself.

My nerves were displeased
by complexity of color
and a suchness
in the angle of each twig.
There was a hectic splendor
and a thickly-matted rendering
that blocked the view
I almost had. Too bad.

And then one day, I can't say why,
it seemed so right in being upright.
No fuss remained; no riot out the window—
instead a simple landscape
noted for the taste with which it wore itself.
The haste of its complexion
had left traces of reflection.
Out there all was Mary
and her necessary way.

XXVII

Anna's Koan: "Mama, are you a Finder and a
Keeper or a Loser and a Weeper?"
I wanted to say, "Anna—I am a
Loser and a Finder"; but instead
I answered as her mother, "A
Finder and a Keeper." So is she.

Emily's Koan: "Mama, which is more—*amen* or
infinity?"

Jessica's Koan: "If we always have to *be* the
way we *are,* how can we be
any *different*?"

Carl's Koan: "Will expanded consciousness
leave stretch marks on the brain
in unelastic minds?"

Marylee's Koan: "Do I praise the Lord with
clashing of symbols?"

Mark's Koan: "How come whenever I go to
bed, you two always start talking about koan somewhere?"

XXVIII

Praying drily, I am called out of bed by my son to come see the orange moon on the horizon. We walk across the meadow (me in nightgown and plastic thongs) as he talks rapidly, energized by the cool air and lately drunk iced tea.

"There she is," he says, pointing me in the right direction. "The orange was deeper before." After a pause, he laughs.

"Oh, how I wish this world would hurry up and end!"

"It'll end soon enough, Mark. What's your hurry?"

"I don't know. Such grand things are coming, I guess."

Gathered together
like a full moon
in the night sky
she encloses her light

Oh my dangerous sun, Jesus,
have mercy!

XXIX

A book like this has plenty of spaces. So does my understanding. So does my talent. But perhaps that's all right because God lies hidden in elliptical places. All my words are trying to say so. Being part of me, they are not yet what they will one day become. Like mummers, all they do is hop around and point.

MARK
MITCHAM

PHOTO CREDITS